CONTENTS

PREFACE

I had been in Singapore just a few days when a young man appeared at my door. "Can I ask you some questions about Buddhism?" he queried. We sat down and began to talk. Some of his questions were similar to the ones that westerners who were just meeting Buddhism would ask. Yet others were peculiar to Asians who had grown up in societies where Buddhism and the old folk religions were often mixed up, at least in the minds of the lay people. As I began teaching in Singapore, I noticed over and over again that the same questions were being asked. Especially the young people, who were intelligent and educated, were earnestly seeking to understand Buddhism and its relationship to modern life.

Soon thereafter, another man came to see me, and in the course of our discussion he said, "We need to hear about Buddha's teachings in everyday English, a clear explanation without a lot of Pali and Sanskrit terms that we do not understand. Why not print a book with some of your talks? I would be happy to help you."

The idea to write this small book thus came from these two people — Lee Siew Cheung and Robert Gwee. My motivation has been to benefit others, although my knowledge is limited and my writing style poor. Any mistakes are due entirely to my own ignorance.

My deepest respect and gratitude is offered to the Buddhas and to my spiritual masters, especially His Holiness the Dalai Lama, Tsenzhab Serkong Rinpoche and Zopa Rinpoche.

Thubten Chodron

THE ESSENCE OF BUDDHISM AND THE BUDDHIST TRADITIONS

What is the essence of the Buddha's teachings?

Simply speaking, this is to avoid harming others and to help them as much as possible. Another way of expressing this is, "Abandon negative action; create perfect virtue; subdue your own mind. This is the teaching of the Buddha." By abandoning negative actions (killing, etc.) and destructive motivations (anger, attachment, close-mindedness, etc.), we stop harming ourselves and others. By creating perfect virtue, we develop beneficial attitudes, like impartial love and compassion, and do actions motivated by these thoughts. By subduing our mind, we cut away all false projections, thus making ourselves calm and peaceful by understanding reality.

The essence of Buddha's teachings is also contained in the three principles of the path: definite emergence, the dedicated heart and wisdom realizing emptiness. Initially, we seek definitely to emerge from the confusion of our problems and their causes. Then, we see that other people also have problems, and with love and compassion, we dedicate our heart to becoming a Buddha so that we are capable of helping others extensively. In order to do this, we develop the wisdom understanding the real nature of ourselves and other phenomena.

What are the Three Jewels? What does it mean to take refuge in them?

The Three Jewels are the Buddha, Dharma and

Sangha. Buddha is one who has purified all the defilements of the mind — the afflictive emotions, the imprints of the actions motivated by them, and the stains of these afflictive emotions — and who has developed all good qualities, such as impartial love and compassion, wisdom knowing all existence, and skilful means of guiding others.

The Dharma embodies the preventive measures which keep us from problems and suffering. This includes the teachings of the Buddha, as well as the realizations of those teachings — the cessations of problems and their causes, and the realizations or paths which lead to those cessations.

The Sangha are those beings who have direct non-conceptual perception of emptiness or ultimate truth. On a relative level, Sangha also refers to the ordained people who put the Buddha's teachings into practice.

The Dharma is our real refuge, the medicine we take which cures our problems and their causes. The Buddha is like the doctor, who correctly diagnoses the cause of our problems and prescribes the appropriate medicine. By assisting us in the practice, the Sangha is similar to the nurse who helps us take the medicine.

Taking refuge means that we rely whole-heartedly on the Three Jewels to inspire and guide us towards a constructive and beneficial direction to take in our life. Taking refuge does not mean passively hiding under the protection of Buddha, Dharma and Sangha. Rather, it is an active process of taking the direction they show and improving the quality of our life.

Why are there many Buddhist traditions?

The Buddha gave a wide variety of teachings because sentient beings (any being with mind who is not a Buddha, including those in other realms of existence) have different dispositions, inclinations and interests. The Buddha never expected us all to fit into the same mold. Thus, he gave many teachings and described various ways of practicing so each of us could find something that suits our level of mind and our personality. With skill and compassion in guiding others, the Buddha turned the wheel of Dharma three times, each time setting forth a slightly different philosophical system in order to suit the various dispositions of sentient beings. The essence of all the teachings is the same: the wish definitely to emerge from the cycle of constantly recurring problems (samsara), compassion for others and the wisdom realizing selflessness.

Not everyone likes the same kind of food. When a huge buffet is spread before us, we choose the dishes that we like. There is no obligation to like everything. Although we may have a taste for sweets, that does not mean that the salty dishes are not good and should be thrown away! Similarly, we may prefer a certain approach to the teachings: Theravada, Pure Land, Zen, Vajrayana, and so on. We are free to choose the approach that suits us best and with which we feel the most comfortable. Yet we still maintain an open mind and respect for other traditions. As our mind develops, we may come to understand elements in other traditions that we failed to comprehend previously. In short, whatever is useful and helps us live a better life, we practice, and whatever we do not yet understand, we leave aside without rejecting it.

While we may find one particular tradition best suited for our personality, do not identify with it in a concrete way: "*I* am a Mahayanist, *you* are a Theravadin," or "*I* am a Buddhist, *you* are a Christian." It is important to remember that we are all human beings seeking happiness and wanting to realize the truth, and we each must find a method suitable for our disposition.

However, keeping an open mind to different approaches does not mean to mix everything together at random, making our practice like chop suey. Do not mix meditation techniques from different traditions together in one meditation session. In one session, it is better to do one technique. If we take a little of this technique and a little from that, and without understanding either one very well mix them together, we may end up confused. However, a teaching emphasized in one tradition may enrich our understanding and practice of another. Also, it is advisable to do the same meditations daily. If we do breathing meditation one day, chanting the Buddha's name the next, and analytical meditation the third, we will not make progress in any of them for there is no continuity in the practice.

What are the various Buddhist traditions?

Generally, there are two divisions: Theravada and Mahayana. The Theravada lineage (Tradition of the Elders), which relies on sutras recorded in the Pali language, spread from India to Sri Lanka, Thailand, Burma, etc. It emphasizes meditation on the breath to develop concentration and meditation on mindfulness of the body, feelings, mind and phenomena in order to develop wisdom. The Mahayana (Great Vehicle) tradition, based on the scriptures recorded in Sanskrit, spread to China, Tibet, Japan, Korea, Vietnam, etc. Although in the Theravadin practice love and compassion are essential and important factors, in the Mahayana they are emphasized to an even greater extent. Within Mahayana, there are several branches: Pure Land emphasizes chanting the name of Amitabha Buddha in order to be reborn in his pure land; Zen emphasizes meditation to eliminate the noisy, conceptual mind; Vajrayana (Diamond Vehicle) employs meditation on a deity in order to transform our contaminated body and mind into the body and mind of a Buddha.

Why do people in some Buddhist traditions eat meat, while those in others are vegetarian?

Initially, it may appear confusing that the Theravadas eat meat, the Chinese Mahayanists do not and the Tibetans, who practice the Vajrayana, do. This difference in practice depends on the different emphasis of each tradition: the emphasis of the Theravadin teachings is to eliminate attachment toward sense objects and to cease the discriminating mind that says,

5

"I like this and not that." Thus, when the monks go out on alms round, they are to accept silently and with gratitude whatever is offered to them, be it meat or not. It would not only offend the benefactors but would also harm a monk's own practice of detachment, if he said, "I cannot eat meat, so give me more of those delicious vegetables." Thus, provided that the meat comes from an animal that the monk neither orders to be killed, nor sees, hears or suspects is killed to give him the meat, he is permitted to eat it. However, it is wise for those who make offerings to remember that the principal premise of Buddhism is not to harm others, and to choose what they offer accordingly.

Upon the foundation of detachment, compassion for other beings is emphasized, especially in the Mahayana tradition. Thus, for such a practitioner it is advisable not to eat meat to avoid inflicting pain on any being and to prevent potential butchers from committing negative actions. Also, because of the vibration of meat, it can impede an ordinary practitioner from developing great compassion. Therefore, vegetarianism is recommended.

The tantric path or Vajrayana has four classes. In the lower classes, external cleanliness and purity are emphasized as a technique for the practitioner to generate internal purity of mind. Therefore, these practitioners do not eat meat, which is regarded as impure. On the other hand, in the highest yoga tantra, on the basis of detachment and compassion, a qualified practitioner does meditation on the subtle nervous system, and for this, one's bodily elements need to be very strong. Thus, meat is recommended for such a person. Also, this class of tantra stresses the transformation of ordinary objects through meditation on selflessness. Such a practitioner, by virtue of his/her profound meditation, is not greedily eating meat for his/her own pleasure.

In Tibet, there is an additional factor to consider: due to the high altitude and harsh climate, there is little to eat besides ground barley, dairy products and meat. To stay alive, the people have to eat meat. His Holiness the Dalai Lama has encouraged those Tibetans in exile, who now live in countries where vegetables and fruits are more plentiful, to refrain from eating meat whenever possible. Also, if a practitioner has severe problems with his/her health due to not eating meat, then the master may give permission to take it. Thus, each person must check his/her own level of practice and bodily requirements and eat accordingly.

The fact that there is such variety within the Buddhist doctrine attests to the Buddha's skill in being able to guide people according to their dispositions and needs. It is extremely important not to be partial and sectarian, but to have respect for all the traditions and their practitioners.

Why do some monks and nuns wear saffron robes while others are dressed in maroon, gray or black?

As the Buddha's teachings spread from one country to another, it was flexible and adapted to the culture and mentality of the people in that place, without changing its essence and meaning. Thus, the style of the Sangha's robes vary. In Sri Lanka, Thailand, Burma, etc., the robes are saffron-colored and without sleeves, like the robes at the time of the Buddha. However, in Tibet dye of that color was not available, so a deeper color, maroon, was used. In China the people considered it rude to expose the skin, so the dress was adapted, the long-sleeved costume of the T'ang Dynasty being used. The culture considered saffron too bright for those on a religious path, so the color was changed to gray. However, the spirit of the original robes was kept in the form of the seven- and nine-pieced brown, yellow and red outer robes.

The way the chanting is done in the various countries is different as well, corresponding to the culture and language of the place. The musical instruments differ too, as does the way of bowing. The Chinese stand up while they chant, the Tibetans sit down. These variations are due to cultural adaptations. It is important to understand that these external forms and ways of doing things are not the Dharma. They are tools to help us practice the Dharma better according to the culture and place in which we live. However, the real Dharma cannot be seen with our eyes or heard with our ears. It is to be experienced by our mind. The real Dharma is what we must emphasize and give our attention to, not superficial appearances which may vary from place to place.

THE BUDDHA

Who is the Buddha? If he is just a man, how can he help us?

There are many ways to describe who the Buddha is, according to different ways of understanding. These various interpretations have their sources in the Buddha's teachings. One way is to see the historical Buddha who lived 2,500 years ago as a human being who cleansed his mind of all defilements and developed all his potential. Any being who does likewise is also considered a Buddha, for there are many Buddhas, not just one. Another way is to understand a particular Buddha or Buddhist deity as the omniscient minds manifesting in a certain physical aspect in order to communicate with us. Yet another way is to see the Buddha — or any of the enlightened Buddhist deities — as the appearance of the future Buddha that we will become once we properly and completely have engaged in the path to cleanse our mind of defilements and develop all of our potential. Let's examine each of these ways in more depth ......

THE HISTORICAL BUDDHA

The historical Buddha, Sakyamuni, was born a prince and had all that life could offer in terms of material possessions and riches, a loving family, fame, reputation and power. He saw that although those things brought temporal worldly happiness, they were never able to bring lasting happiness. Thus, he left the princely environment to become an ascetic searching for truth. After doing severe physical austerities for six years, he saw that the extreme of self-denial also was not the path to ultimate happiness. At this point, he sat under the bodhi tree, and in deep meditation completely purified his mind of all wrong conceptions, contaminated actions and their imprints, and brought to perfection all of his potential and good qualities. He then proceeded with great compassion, wisdom and skill, to give teachings, thus enabling others to gradually purify their mind, develop their potential, and attain the same realizations and state of happiness that he had.

How can such a person save us from our problems and pain? Certainly he cannot pull out the afflictive emotions from our mind in the same way as a thorn can be extracted from someone's foot. Nor can he wash away our defilements with water, or pour his realizations into our minds. The Buddha has impartial compassion to all sentient beings and cherishes us more than himself, so if our sufferings could have been eliminated by only the action of the Buddha, he would have done it already.

However, our experience, our happiness or pain, depends on our mind. It depends on whether or not we assume the responsibility to subdue our afflictive emotions and actions. The Buddha showed the method to do this, the method that he himself used to go from the state of an ordinary confused being like we are now to the state of total purification and growth, or Buddhahood. It is up to us to practice this method and transform our own mind. Sakyamuni Buddha is someone who did what we want to do — to reach a state of lasting happiness.

He taught that by means of both his life story and the various teachings he gave. But he cannot control our minds, only we can. Our enlightenment depends not only on the Buddha showing us the way, but on our own efforts to follow it.

It is like if we want to go to London. First we find out if such a place called London actually exists, and then we look for someone who has been there and who has the knowledge and capability and willingness to give us all of the travel information. It would be foolish to follow someone who had never been there, because he/she could unwittingly make a mistake in the explanation. Likewise, the Buddha has attained the state of total purification and growth; he has the wisdom, compassion and skill to show us the path. It would be silly to entrust ourselves to the guidance of someone who had not reached the enlightened state him/herself.

Our travel guide can give us information about what to take with on our trip and what to leave behind. He/she can tell us how to change planes, how to recognise the various places we will pass through, what dangers we could encounter along the way and so forth. Similarly, the Buddha has described the various levels of the paths and stages, how to progress from one to the next, what qualities to take with us and develop, and which ones to leave behind. However, a travel guide cannot force us to make the journey — he/she can only indicate the way. We have to get ourselves to the airport and on the plane. Just so, the Buddha cannot force us to practice the path. He gives the teachings and shows by his example how to do it, but we have to do it ourselves.

THE BUDDHAS AS MANIFESTATIONS

The second way to think of the Buddhas is as manifestations of omniscient minds in a physical form. Those beings who are Buddhas are omniscient in that they perceive all existent phenomena as clearly as we can see the palm of our hand. They achieved this ability by fully developing their wisdom and compassion, thus eliminating all defects. But we cannot communicate directly with the Buddhas' omniscient minds as we have no clairvoyance. In order for the Buddhas to fulfil their most heartfelt wish to lead all sentient beings to enlightenment, they have to communicate with us, and in order to do so, they assume a physical form. In this way, we can think of Sakyamuni Buddha as a being who was already enlightened, and who appeared in the aspect of a prince in order to teach us.

But if he is already enlightened, how can he take rebirth? Shakyamuni did not take rebirth under the control of afflictive emotions and contaminated actions (karma) as ordinary beings do, as he had already eliminated these defilements from his mind. However, he was able to appear on this earth by the power of compassion.

When thinking of the Buddha as a manifestation, do not emphasize the Buddha as a personality. Rather, concentrate on the qualities of the onmniscient mind appearing in the form of a person. This is a more abstract way of understanding the Buddha, so it takes more effort on our part to think in this way and to understand.

In the same way, the various enlightened Buddhist deities can be seen as manifestations of the omniscient minds. Why are there so many deities if all the beings who have attained enlightenment have the same realizations? This is because each physical appearance emphasizes and communicates with different aspects of our personality. This demonstrates the Buddhas' skillful means. For example, Avalokiteshvara (Kuan Yin, Chenresig) is the manifestation of the compassion of all the Buddhas. Although possessing all the compassion and wisdom of any Buddha, Avalokiteshvara's particular manifestation emphasizes compassion. By thinking of, praying to and meditating on Avalokiteshvara, we can develop all the qualities of the Buddhas, and especially our compassion will develop more quickly.

The white color of Avalokiteshvara emphasizes purity, in this case the purification of selfishness through compassion. The thousand arms, each with an eye in its palm, expresses how impartial compassion looks upon all beings and is willing to reach out to help them. By visualizing compassion in this physical aspect, we communicate with compassion in a non-verbal and symbolic way.

Manjushri is the manifestation of the wisdom of all the Buddhas, although Manjushri, too, has the same realizations as all the Buddhas. Manjushri, as found in the Tibetan tradition, is depicted as yellow in color, holding a flaming sword and a lotus flower with the *Perfection of Wisdom Sutra*. This physical form is symbolic of inner realizations. Yellow color represents wisdom, which illuminates the mind just as golden rays of the sun light up the earth. The sword, too, represents wisdom in its function of cutting ignorance. Holding the *Perfection of Wisdom Sutra* indicates that the way we are to develop wisdom is by studying, contemplating and meditating on this sutra. By visualizing and meditating on Manjushri, we can attain the qualities of a Buddha, especially wisdom.

In this way we can understand why there are so many deities. Each emphasizes a particular aspect of the enlightened qualities, in order to communicate that quality to us symbolically. That does not mean, however, that there is no such being as Avalokiteshvara, for on one level, we can understand the Buddha of Compassion to be a person residing in a certain Pure Land. On another level, we can see him (or her) as a manifestation of compassion in a physical form. Do not get confused because Avalokiteshvara is sometimes in a male form and sometimes in a female form. It is not because he/she could not make up his/her mind! The enlightened mind is actually beyond being male or female. These are just appearances in order to communicate with us ordinary beings who are so involved in forms. An enlightened being can appear in a wide variety of bodies.

The nature of all these various manifestations is the same: the omniscient mind of wisdom and compassion. All of the Buddhas and deities are not separate beings in the same way that an apple and an orange are separate fruits. Rather, they all have the same nature, only they appear in different external forms in order to communicate with us in different ways. From one lump of clay, a pot, a vase, a plate, or a figurine can be made. The nature of all of them is the same — clay — yet they perform different functions according to how the clay is shaped. In the same way, the nature of all the Buddhas and deities is the omniscient mind of wisdom and compassion. This appears in a variety of forms in order to perform various functions. Thus, when we want to develop compassion, we emphasize meditation on Avalokiteshvara; when our mind is dull and sluggish, we emphasize the practice of Manjushri, the Buddha of Wisdom. These Buddhas all have the same realizations, yet each one has his/her speciality.

THE BUDDHA THAT WE WILL BECOME

The third way to understand the Buddha that we take refuge in is as the appearance of our own Buddha nature in its fully developed form. All sentient beings have the potential to become Buddhas, for we all have the clear nature of the mind. At the present our mind is clouded by afflictive emotions (klesa) and actions (karma). Through constant practice, we can remove these defilements from our mind stream and nourish the seeds of all the beautiful potentials we have. Thus, each of us can become a Buddha when this process of purification and growth is completed. This is a feature unique to Buddhism, for in most other religions there is an irreparable gap between the divine being and the human being. However, the Buddha said that each sentient being has the potential for perfection. It is only a matter of engaging in the practice and creating the causes to reach perfection.

When we visualize the Buddha or a deity and think of

him/her as the future Buddha that we will become, we are imagining our now latent Buddha nature in its completely developed form. We are thinking of the future time when we shall have completed the path of purification and growth. We are imagining the future in the present, and in this way reaffirming our own latent goodness. This also helps us to understand that what ultimately protects us from suffering is our own practice and achievement of enlightenment.

These different ways of understanding the Buddha are progressively more difficult to understand. We may not grasp them immediately. That is alright. Various interpretations are explained because people have different ways of understanding. We are not expected to all think in the same way or to understand everything at once.

IDOLS AND OFFERINGS

Do Buddhists worship idols?

Not at all! A piece of clay or bronze or jade is not the object of our respect and worship. When we bow before Buddha images, we are recalling the qualities of the enlightened beings. It is their impartial love and compassion, generosity, morality, patience, joyous effort, concentration and wisdom that we are showing respect to. The statue or painting serves to remind us of the qualities of the Buddha, and it is the qualities, not the clay, that we are bowing to. We need not have a statue in front of us in order to bow to or respect the Buddhas and their qualities.

For example, if we go to a place far away from our family, we think about them and feel much love. But we also like to have a photo of them with us to remember them better. When we look at the photo and feel love for our family, we are not loving the paper and ink of the photo! The photo merely strengthens our memory. It is similar with a statue or painting of the Buddha.

By showing respect to the Buddhas and their qualities, we are inspired to develop these extraordinary qualities on our own mind streams. We become like the people we respect. When we take the loving-kindness and wisdom of the Buddhas as our example, we strive to become like them.

What is the purpose of making offerings to the Buddha?

We do not make offerings because the Buddha needs our offerings. When someone has purified all defilements and enjoys the bliss that comes from wisdom, he/she certainly does not need an incense stick to be happy! Neither do we make offerings to win the Buddha's favor. The Buddha developed impartial love and compassion long ago and will not be swayed by flattery and bribery like ordinary beings! Making offerings is a way to create positive potential and to develop our mind. At the moment, we have excessive attachment and miserliness. We keep the biggest and best for ourselves and give the second best or something we do not want at all to others. With such selfish traits, we always feel poor and dissatisfied, no matter how much we have. We constantly fear losing what little we do have. Such an attitude towards material objects makes our mind restless, and induces us to do dishonest actions to get more things or to be unkind to others in order to protect what we have.

It is to break these destructive habits of attachment and miserliness that we make offerings. When making an offering, we want to do so without any feeling of loss from our side. It is for this reason that in the Tibetan tradition, seven bowls of water are offered on the altar. Water is readily accessible so that we can easily offer it without attachment or miserliness. By offering in this way, we habituate ourselves with the thought and action of giving. Thus, we come to feel rich when we give and take pleasure in sharing good things with others.

Since the Buddhas, bodhisattvas and arhats are the highest of all beings, it is good to make offerings to them. We usually give offerings to our friends because we like them. Here, we offer to the holy beings because we are attracted to their qualities. We should not make offerings with a motivation to bribe the Buddhas, "I offered you incense, now you are obliged to grant my prayers"! We give with a respectful and kind attitude. If later, we make a request, we do so with humility. Do not think that they do not receive the offerings just because the flowers and fruit are still on the altar the next day. They can receive them without taking them away.

Is there symbolic meaning to each offering substance?

Yes. Flowers represent the qualities of the Buddhas and bodhisattvas, incense the fragrance of pure morality. Light symbolizes wisdom, and perfume represents faith. Offering food is like offering the nourishment of meditative concentration and music symbolizes impermanence and the empty nature of all phenomena.

While we may physically offer one flower, mentally we can imagine the entire sky filled with beautiful flowers and offer these as well. It enriches our mind to imagine lovely things and then offer them to the Buddhas and bodhisattvas.

Should we offer our food before eating it?

Yes. Normally we just dive into a plate of food

with much attachment, little mindfulness, and even less real enjoyment. Now, we pause before eating and imagine the food as blissful nectar. This is offered to a small Buddha made of light in our heart center (chakra). The Buddha enjoys the nectar and he radiates even more light which fills our entire body and makes us very blissful. In this way, we remain mindful of the Buddha and of the process of eating. We create positive potential by offering to the Buddha, and we also enjoy the food more.

Before eating, some people like to recite the prayer: "May we and those around us never be separated from the Three Jewels (Buddha, Dharma and Sangha) in all future lives. May we continuously make offerings to the Three Jewels and may we receive the inspiration of the Three Jewels."

PRAYER AND DEDICATING POSITIVE POTENTIAL

Why make prayers? Can they be fulfilled?

There are many kinds of prayers. Some are to direct and inspire our mind towards a certain quality or aim, thus creating the cause for us to attain this. An example is praying to be more tolerant and compassionate towards others. Other prayers are for specific people or situations, as in praying for a certain person's illness to be cured. To have either type of prayer fulfilled depends on more than just praying: the appropriate causes must also be created. It is not just a matter of saying, "Please, Buddha, make this and that happen, but I'm going to relax and have tea while you do the work!"

For example, if we pray to be more loving and compassionate and yet make no effort to control our anger, we are not creating the cause for that prayer to be fulfilled. The transformation of our mind comes from our own effort, and we pray for the Buddhas' inspiration to do so. "Receiving the blessings of the Buddhas" does not mean that something tangible comes from the Buddhas and goes into us. It means that our mind is transformed through the combined effort of the teachings and guidance of the Buddhas and Bodhisattvas and our own practice. Thus, we cannot pray to be born in a pure land and expect the Buddhas and Bodhisattvas to do all the work! We must also make effort to actualize the teachings: we gradually develop detachment from worldly pleasures, we practice compassion as much as we can, and we generate wisdom. Then, praying

21

has an exceptionally profound effect on our mind. However, if we do nothing to correct our bad habits of body, speech and mind, and if our mind is distracted while praying, then there is minimal effect.

As for our prayers for a sickness to be cured or the family finances to improve or for a deceased relative to have a good rebirth, these, too, depend on the person involved having created the necessary causes. If he/she has, our prayers provide the condition for the seed of a virtuous action he/she did in the past to ripen and bring its result. However, if that person has not created the causal seed through his/her own positive past actions, then it is difficult for our prayers to be fulfilled. We can put fertilizer and water on the ground, but if the farmer has not planted the seed, nothing will grow.

While describing how cause and effect works in our mental continuum, the Buddha said that killing causes shortness of life. Both abandoning killing and saving others' lives cause us to have a long life, free from illness. If we neglect to follow this basic advice and yet pray to have a long and healthy life, we are missing the point! On the other hand, if in the past the person concerned has abandoned killing and has saved lives, then prayers for him/her could be fulfilled.

In the same way, the Buddha said generosity is the cause of wealth. If we have been generous in a past life and now pray for our wealth to increase, then our finances could improve. Yet, if we are very miserly now, we are creating the cause for poverty, not wealth, in the future. Being generous, helping those in need and sharing what we have, will bring their desirable results sometime in the future. On the other hand, when we experience some difficulties in our life, it is good to ask ourselves, "What kind of action could I have done that created the cause for this result?" This we can learn from the Buddha's teachings. Then we can change our behavior to avoid leaving more seeds to experience that undesirable result.

What role does chanting play in our spiritual development?

Chanting can be very beneficial if engaged in with the proper motivation — wishing to prepare for future lives, striving for liberation from the cycle of constantly recurring problems, or aiming for the full enlightenment of a Buddha with an altruistic motivation. Also, for chanting to be effective in helping us to generate positive states of mind, we need to concentrate and reflect upon the meaning of what we are chanting. There is not much benefit if we chant while our mind is thinking about food or work or parties. A tape recorder can also chant the names of the Buddhas and say prayers! Let's make what our mind is thinking correspond to what our mouth is chanting. Then chanting is very powerful and beneficial.

However, a complete spiritual practice is more than just chanting. It is good to listen to teachings, contemplate their meaning and integrate them into our daily life, thus developing beneficial actions with our body, speech and mind. We cannot be liberated from samsara by chanting alone, for deep meditation is necessary in order to generate the wisdom realising selflessness.

Can merits be transferred to deceased ones?

"Dedicate" rather than "transfer" merits (positive potential) conveys the meaning better. We cannot transfer merits in the same way as we can transfer the title to a piece of property or in the same way as I give my car to you because you do not have one. The Buddha stated that those who create the causes are the ones who experience the results. I cannot create the cause and you experience the result, because the imprint or seed of the action has been implanted on my mental continuum, not yours. So if the deceased ones did not create positive actions while they were alive, we cannot create the good karma and then give them our good karma to experience.

However, our prayers and offerings on their behalf can create the circumstances necessary so that a positive action they created can bear its fruit. When a seed is planted in a field, it needs the cooperative conditions of sunshine, water and fertilizer to grow. Likewise, a seed or imprint of an action a person performed will ripen when all the cooperative conditions are present. If the deceased one has done beneficial actions while he/she was alive, then the additional positive potential we create by making offerings or doing any kind of virtuous action — reciting and reading Dharma texts, making statues of the Buddha, contemplating love and compassion for all beings and so forth — can help them. We dedicate the positive potential from these actions for the benefit of the deceased person, and this could help his/her own virtuous seeds to ripen.

What is merit? Isn't it selfish to do positive actions just to get merit, as if it were spiritual money?

"Merit" is an English word that does not really give the correct connotation. It sounds like getting gold stars in school because you did well, and that is not the meaning intended here. First of all, no one is rewarding us. When we do a beneficial action, it leaves an imprint or seed on our mental continuum, and when the necessary cooperative conditions are present, it will bear fruit. It is not a physical seed or imprint, but an intangible one, a positive potential.

It is not very advantageous to grasp at positive potential as if it were spiritual money. If we do, we are likely to quarrel with other people over who can make offerings first or become jealous of others because they do more virtuous actions than we do. Such attitudes are certainly not very beneficial! While it is good to take advantage of opportunities to create positive potential, we should do so in order to improve ourselves, to create the cause for happiness and to help others, not out of attachment or jealousy.

Why must positive potential be dedicated? What should it be dedicated for?

It is important to dedicate our positive potential so it does not get destroyed by our anger or wrong views. Like the steering wheel guiding where the car goes, dedication will guide how our positive potential ripens. It is best to dedicate for the most extensive and noble goals. If we do so, all the smaller results will naturally come. If we set our destination as London, we will pass through Delhi and Kuwait along the way; we do not need a special ticket for those places. Likewise, if we dedicate our positive potential, however small, towards the ultimate happiness and enlightenment of all sentient beings, this automatically includes dedicating for a good rebirth and for the happiness of our relatives and friends.

Some people think, "I have so little positive potential. If I dedicate it for the happiness of everyone, then I won't have any left over for myself." This is not correct. By dedicating our positive potential to others, it does not mean that we have less for ourselves. We will not become paupers by sharing the good results of our actions with others. While dedicating our positive potential for the benefit of all beings, we can still make special prayers, for the happiness of a particular person who is having difficulties at that time.

REBIRTH VS. CREATION

What is rebirth?

Rebirth refers to a person's mind taking one body after the other. Our body and our mind are separate entities: the body is matter and is made of atoms. The mind refers to all of our emotional and cognitive experiences, and is formless. When the body and mind are linked, we are alive, but at death, they separate. The body becomes a corpse, and the mind continues on to take another body.

How did our mind begin? Who or what created it?

Each moment of mind is a continuation of the previous moment: who we are and what we think and feel depends on who we were yesterday. Our present mind is a continuation of yesterday's mind. That is why we can remember what happened to us in the past. One moment of our mind is caused by the previous moment of our mind. This continuity can be traced back to childhood and even to our mind when we were a fetus inside our mother's womb. Even before the time of conception, our mind stream existed: its previous moments were linked to another body.

There was no beginning to our mind. Who said there had to be a beginning? The continuity of our mind is infinite. This may be a difficult concept to grasp initially, but if we use the example of a number line, it becomes easier. From the "0" position, looking left, there is no first negative number, and looking right, there is no last, highest number. One more can always be added on. In the same way, our mind stream has no beginning and no end. We all have had an infinite number of past rebirths, and our mind will continue to exist infinitely. However, by purifying our mind stream, we can make our future existences better than our present one.

In fact, it would be impossible for our mind stream to have a beginning. As each moment of mind is caused by its previous moment, if there were a beginning, then that would mean that the first moment of mind either had no cause or it was caused by something else besides a previous moment of mind. But both of those alternatives are impossible, for mind can only be produced by a previous moment of mind in its own continuum.

What connects one life with the next? Is there a soul, atman, self, or real personality that goes from one life to another?

Our mind has gross and subtle levels. The sense consciousnesses that see, hear, smell, taste and feel tactile sensations, and the gross mental consciousness, which is always so busy thinking this and that, function very actively while we are alive. At the time of death, they cease to function and absorb into the subtle mental consciousness. This subtle mind bears with it all the imprints of the actions we have done. It is this subtle mind which leaves one body, enters the intermediate state and finally takes rebirth in another body. After the subtle mind is joined with another body at the moment of conception, the gross sense consciousnesses and the gross mental consciousness reappear, and the person again sees, hears, thinks, etc. This subtle mind, which goes from one life to the next, is a constantly changing phenomena. For this reason, it is not considered to be a soul, atman, self or real personality. Thus, the Buddha taught the doctrine of selflessness.

How was the world created?

Anything that is created arises from causes that were able to produce it. Something cannot be created out of nothing. The physical world of forms was produced by previous moments of form. Science is investigating this. They may find that at the beginning of our particular universe, there were subtler physical elements from which our present universe was created. These subtler physical elements, in turn, were a continuation from universes which existed prior to ours. Thus, we can trace the continuity of form back infinitely.

Why can't we remember our past lives?

At the moment, our mind is obscured by ignorance, making it difficult to remember the past. Also, many changes occur in our body and mind as we die and are reborn, making recollection difficult. However, the fact that we do not remember something, does not mean that it does not exist. Sometimes we cannot even remember where we put our car keys! Nor can we remember what we ate for dinner a month ago!

There are people who can remember their past lives. In the Tibetan community, there is a system of recognizing the reincarnations of highly realized masters. Quite often, as young children, these people will recognize their friends or possessions from a previous life. Some ordinary people, too, have had past life recall, perhaps in meditation or through hypnosis.

Is it important to know what our past lives were?

No. What is important is how we live our present life. Knowing what we were in past lives is only useful if it helps us to generate strong determination to avoid negative actions and definitely to emerge from the cycle of constantly recurring problems. To try to find out who we were in past lives only for curiosity's sake is not useful. It could even lead us to become proud: "Oh I was a king in my past life. I was so famous and talented. I was Einstein!" So what?! Actually, we have all been and done everything in many past lives in this cycle of existence. What is important is that now we purify our previously created negative potentials, avoid creating more, and put energy into accumulating positive potential and developing our good qualities.

There is a Tibetan saying, "If you want to know about your past life, look at your present body. If you want to know your future life, look at your present mind." We received the rebirth we now have as a result of our past actions. A human rebirth is a fortunate rebirth and the cause for it was created by our having guarded our morality well in past lives. On the other hand, our future rebirths will be determined by the actions we perform now, and it is the mind which motivates all of our other actions. Thus, by looking at our present attitudes and examining whether they are virtuous or non-virtuous, we can get an idea of the kind of rebirths we will take. We do not need to go to a fortune teller to ask what will become of us: we simply look at what imprints we are leaving on our mental continuum by the actions we are doing.

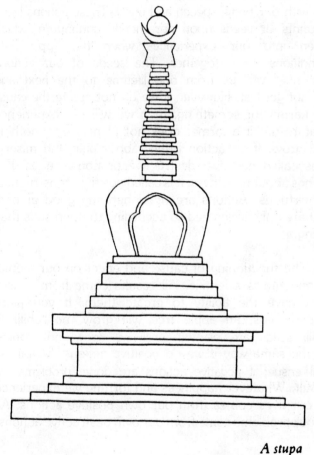

A stupa

KARMA: THE FUNCTIONING OF CAUSE AND EFFECT

What is karma? How does it work?

Karma means action, and refers to actions that we do with our body, speech and mind. These actions leave imprints or seeds upon our mental continuum, which ripen into our experiences when the appropriate conditions come together. The seeds of our actions continue with us from one lifetime to the next and do not get lost. However, if we do not create the cause or karma for something, then we will not experience that result: if a farmer does not plant seeds, nothing will grow. If an action brings about pain and misery, it is called negative, destructive or non-virtuous. If it brings about happiness, it is called positive, constructive, or virtuous. Actions are not inherently good or bad, but are only designated so according to the results they bring.

The functioning of cause and effect on our mental continuum is scientific. All results come from causes that have the ability to create them. If you plant apple seeds, an apple tree will grow, not chilli. If chilli seeds are planted, chilli will grow, not apples. In the same way if we do positive actions, happiness will ensue; if negative actions are done, problems will result. Whatever happiness and fortune we experience in our lives comes from our own positive actions. All of our problems come from our own destructive actions.

Is karma or the law of cause and effect a system of punishment and reward? Did the Buddha create or invent the law of cause and effect?

Definitely not. There is no one who distributes rewards and punishments. We create the causes by our actions, and we experience their results. We are responsible for our own experience. Nor did Buddha create the system of cause and effect, in the same way that Newton did not invent gravity. Buddha merely described what he saw through the power of his omniscient mind to be the natural process of cause and effect that is happening within the mental continuum of each sentient being. By doing this, he showed us how best to work within the law of cause and effect in order to get the happiness we desire and avoid the pain we dislike.

The misconception that happiness and pain are rewards and punishments may come from incorrect translations of Buddhist scriptures into English. I have seen some texts translated into English using terminology from other religions. This is very misleading. Terms such as "heaven," "hell," "sin," "punishment," "judgement," and so forth, do not at all explain Buddhist concepts. Appropriate English words which convey the meaning of the Buddha's teachings should be used.

Does the law of cause and effect apply only to people who believe in it?

No. Cause and effect functions whether we accept it or not. Positive actions produce happiness and destructive ones pain whether we believe in it or not. If a fruit drops from a tree, it falls down even if we believe it will go up. It would be wonderful if all we needed to do to avoid the results of our actions is not believe they will come! Then we could eat all we want and never get fat! A person who does not believe in past lives and cause and effect can still experience happiness as a result of his actions in past lives. By denying the existence of cause and effect, and consequently not making an effort to practice constructive actions and avoid destructive ones, the person creates few positive potentials and recklessly creates many negative ones. On the other hand, people who know about cause and effect will make effort to be mindful of what they think, say and do to avoid hurting others and to avoid leaving harmful imprints on their own mental continuum.

Why are some people who commit many negative actions successful and appear to be happy? Why do some people who do not believe in the functioning of cause and effect have good lives?

When we see dishonest people having wealth, or cruel people receiving respect and power, or kind people being robbed or dying young, we may doubt the law of cause and effect. This is because we are only looking at what is happening in the short period of time of this one life. Many of the results we experience in this life are results of actions created in previous lives, and many of the actions we perform in this life will ripen only in future lives. The wealth of dishonest people is the result of their generosity in preceding lives. Their current dishonesty is leaving the karmic seed for them to be cheated and to experience poverty in future lives. Likewise, the respect and authority given to cruel people is due to positive actions they did in the past. In the present, they are misusing their power, thus creating the cause for future pain. Kind people who die young are experiencing the result of negative actions such as killing done in past lives. However, their present kindness is planting seeds or imprints on the mental continuum for them to have happiness in the future.

The exact way in which a specific action ripens and what particular actions we did in the past to bring a specific result in our life can only be known completely by the Buddha's omniscient mind. What is stated in the sutras and tantras about a certain action bringing a certain result is a general guideline. However, in specific situations, things may vary a bit depending on other causes and conditions. That destructive actions bring pain and constructive ones bring happiness does not change. But in a particular situation of an individual, a negative action of, for example, killing may ripen in any of the lower forms of rebirth. This depends on many factors which could make that action heavy or light, as well as on the conditions present at the time when that karmic seed is ripening.

Do we necessarily experience the results of all of our actions?

When seeds, even small ones, are planted in the ground, they eventually will sprout; that is, unless they do not receive the conditions such as water, sunshine and fertilizer necessary for their growth, or unless they are burnt or pulled out of the ground. The ultimate way of uprooting the karmic imprints or seeds is by meditation on the emptiness of inherent existence. This is the way to purify the afflictive emotions and the karmic imprints completely. At our level, this is rather difficult, but we still can stop the harmful imprints from ripening by doing purification. This is similar to keeping the seed from receiving water, sunshine and fertilizer.

How can we purify negative imprints?

Purification by means of the four opponent powers is very important. It not only prevents future suffering, but also relieves the guilt or the heavy feeling we experience now. By cleansing our mind, we are able to understand the Dharma better, and we are more peaceful and can concentrate better. The four opponent powers used to purify negative imprints or seeds are:

1) regret,
2) determination not to do the action again,
3) taking refuge and generating an altruistic attitude toward others,
4) an actual remedial practice.

First, we acknowledge and have regret for doing the destructive action. Self-recrimination and guilt are quite useless and are just a way of emotionally torturing ourselves. With sincere regret, on the other hand, we acknowledge that we made a mistake and regret doing it.

Secondly, we make a determination not to do the action again. If it is an action that we do habitually and frequently, like criticizing others, it would be hypocritical to say we will never do that again the rest of our lives. It is better to choose a realistic amount of time and determine that we will try not to repeat the action, but will be especially mindful and make concerted effort during that period of time.

The third opponent power is that of reliance. Our destructive actions are generally in relation to either holy objects such as Buddha, Dharma and Sangha, or other sentient beings. To reestablish a good relationship with the holy objects we rely on them by taking refuge or seeking direction from them. To have a good relationship with other sentient beings we generate an altruistic attitude toward them so that we dedicate our heart to becoming Buddha in order to be able to benefit them in the best way.

The fourth element is to do a remedial action. This may be any positive action: listening to teachings, reading a Dharma book, prostrating, making offerings, reciting the names of the Buddhas, chanting mantras, making statues or paintings of the Buddhas, printing texts, meditating and so on. The most powerful remedial action is to meditate on emptiness.

The four opponent powers must be done repeatedly. We have done negative actions many times, so naturally we cannot expect to counteract them all at once. The stronger the four opponents powers are — the stronger our regret is, the firmer our determination not to do the action again is, and so on — the more powerful the purification will be. It is very good to do purification with the four opponent powers every evening before going to sleep in order to counteract whatever destructive actions we may have committed during the day.

If people suffer because of their own negative actions, does that mean that we cannot or should not do anything to help them?

Not at all! We know what it is like to feel miserable, and that is exactly how another person who is experiencing the results of his own destructive actions feels. Out of empathy and compassion, we should definitely help! That person's present predicament was caused by his/her own actions, but that does not mean that we stand by and relax say, "Oh that's too bad. You poor thing. You shouldn't have done such non-virtuous actions."

Do not think of karma in an inflexible way. Yes, that person created the cause to experience that difficulty by his/her own actions, but maybe he/she also created the cause to receive help from us! But even more than that, we all know what we would feel like if it were us in that horrible situation. We are all alike in wanting happiness and not wanting pain. It does not matter whose pain or problem it is, it should be removed. To think, "The poor are poor because of their own past lives' miserliness. I would be interfering with the natural process of cause and effect if I tried to help," is a complete misconception. We should not try to rationalize our own laziness or apathy or attachment to our superior position by misinterpreting cause and effect. A sense of compassion and universal responsibility are important for our own spiritual development and for world peace.

IMPERMANENCE AND SUFFERING

In Buddhism, there is much emphasis on impermanence, death and suffering. Isn't such an approach to life unhealthy?

The purpose of contemplating impermanence, death and suffering is not to become depressed and have the joy taken out of life. The purpose is to rid ourselves of attachment and false expectations. If we contemplate these things in such a way that we get emotionally afraid or depressed, then we are not contemplating in the right way. Rather, such subjects should make our mind calm and more lucid as the confusion caused by attachment has been ceased.

At the moment, our mind is easily overwhelmed with the false projections of attachment. We see people and objects in an unrealistic way. Things that are changing moment by moment appear to us to be constant and unchanging. That is why we are upset when they break. We may say, "All these things are impermanent," but our words are not consistent with our innate view which considers our body and so on as unchanging phenomena. Our unrealistic conception is what causes pain, because we have expectations of things and people that cannot be fulfilled. Our loved ones cannot live forever; a relationship does not remain the same, the new car will not always be the shiny model just off the showroom floor. Thus, we are perpetually disappointed when we must part with those we care about, when our possessions break, when our body becomes weak or wrinkled. If we had a more realistic view of these things from the beginning and accepted their impermanence — not just from our mouth but with our heart — then such disappointment would not come.

Contemplating impermanence and death also eliminates much of the useless worries that plague us and prevent us from being happy and relaxed. Ordinarily, we become very upset when we are criticized or insulted. We are angry when our possessions are stolen; we are jealous if someone else gets the promotion we wanted; we are proud of our looks or athletic ability. All of these attitudes are afflictive emotions which leave harmful imprints on our mental continuum that bring us problems in the future lives. Even in this life, we are not happy. However, if we contemplate how transcient these things are, if we remember that our life will definitely end and that none of these things can accompany us at death, then we stop exaggerating their importance now. They cease to become so problematic to us.

That does not mean that we become apathetic towards the people and things around us. On the contrary, by eliminating the wrong conception of permanence and the afflictive emotions which arise depending on it, our mind becomes clearer and more capable of enjoying things for what they are. We live more in the present, appreciating things as they are now, without fantasies about what they are or will be. We worry less about small matters and are less distracted when we sit down to meditate. We become less ego-sensitive to every action other people do in relation to us. By reflecting on impermanence and suffering, we can deal better with separation and pain when they occur, and occur they will as we are still in the cycle of constantly recurring problems. In short, by correctly contemplating these truths, our mental state becomes healthier.

Why is there suffering? How do we stop it?

Suffering occurs simply because the causes for it exist: afflictive emotions — ignorance, attachment, anger and so on — and the actions we do motivated by these misconceptions, such as killing, stealing, lying and so forth. By developing the wisdom realising selfless-ness, we stop the causes of our problems. Then the painful results cannot follow, and instead, we can abide in a state of lasting happiness or nirvana. In the meantime, before we generate that wisdom, we can do purification practices in order to prevent the previously created destructive actions from bringing their results.

The Buddha also taught many skilful ways to think in order to transform difficult circumstances into the path to enlightenment. We can learn about these and practice them whenever we have problems.

Do we have to suffer in order to attain liberation (nirvana)?

Practicing Buddha's teachings brings happiness and never pain. The spiritual path is not itself painful. There is no special virtue in suffering. We already have enough problems, so there is no reason to cause ourselves more in the name of practicing religion. However, that does not mean that while we are endeavoring to practice the Dharma that we will have no problems. For while we are on the path, previously created destructive actions that have not yet been purified may ripen and bring problems. If and when this happens, we must use the situation to energize ourselves to practice better so as to reach a state beyond suffering, a state of lasting happiness.

DEATH

How can we best help someone who is dying or dead?

When a person is dying, it is best that the environment be calm. Reassure the dying person that his/her worldly affairs will be taken care of after he/she passes away. There is no need to be concerned over who will pay the bills or who will take care of the children. It is better to concentrate on leaving this life peacefully, without fears or worries. Don't bother the person by asking, "Who will get your jewelry?" "Do you have any hidden money?" "How will I survive without you?" Our motivation is to help the dying person, not give him/her more problems!

It is difficult to die peacefully if the whole family is in the room crying, wailing and grasping the person's hand, and saying, "Please don't die. I love you. How can you leave me alone?" We may think we are expressing our love and concern by such emotional displays, but actually, it is just our own selfish mind wailing because we are losing someone we care about. If we really cared about the dying person more than ourselves, we would try to make the environment calm and pleasant. We would try to be sensitive to the other's requests and needs, not our own.

It is harmful to die with anger or attachment, jealousy or pride as one's last thought. It is for this reason that we try to make the environment quiet and calm and encourage the person to generate positive thoughts.

If the person is Buddhist, we can talk about the Buddha, Dharma and Sangha. Tell him/her to remember his/her spiritual master and the Buddha. We can show him/her a picture of the Buddha or chant some prayers and mantras in the room. Before death actually occurs, if we can guide the person to make confession and purify non-virtuous actions, it is very beneficial. Encourage him/her to pray for a good rebirth, to meet pure teachings and teachers and make the life beneficial for others.

On the other hand, if a person is of another faith, at the time of death, it is unwise to push our faith on him/her. That could cause confusion. It is best to speak according to that person's faith and to encourage the generation of positive states of mind.

Does chanting for the dead help? What else can be done for them?

After death, chanting the sutras and doing other Buddhist practices can be helpful in terms of acting as a cooperative condition for the person's own positive potential to ripen. The person has already left that body and does not hear the chanting with his/her ears. Nevertheless, by the power of strong dedication, our creating positive potential can help. Also, each week for seven weeks after death, it is helpful to do such chanting. This is because if the person has not already found another gross body to take rebirth in, he/she is still in the intermediate stage, the stage between the death of one gross body and the assumption of another. The positive potential we create and dedicate for the deceased can help him/her find a good rebirth. However, do not think, "I'll ask some monks and nuns to do the chanting while I go to play majong." We have a karmic relationship with the deceased, so our prayers and our virtuous activities which are dedicated for that person's benefit are important too.

It is good to offer the deceased's possessions to others as a way of performing generosity and accumulating positive potential. Offering to holy objects — Buddha, Dharma, Sangha — and to needy people — the poor and sick — is beneficial as well. The positive potential from this is then dedicated for the benefit of all sentient beings and especially for that person.

Is it necessary to leave food out for the deceased? What about burning paper money and so forth for them?

After a person's mind leaves this gross body, it enters the intermediate stage before it assumes another gross body. Depending on conditions, a person may remain in the intermediate stage only a few moments, or as long as forty-nine days. It is said that intermediate state beings survive by "eating" smells, so leaving out food may be helpful. According to his/her previous actions, the person is reborn in a happy or painful transmigration. If our relative has been born as a god (deva), human, animal or other type of rebirth, the food set out never reaches him/her, and most likely, there is food available in that realm. If he/she has been reborn as a hungry ghost, there are certain mantras to be recited over the food, which can eliminate the karmic obscurations of hungry ghosts to finding food.

Burning paper cars or clothes or money does not give the deceased these things in their future rebirth. It is not necessary to burn all these things. The tradition of doing so is an old Chinese custom, not a practice taught by the Buddha. If we really want to help our relatives and friends to have wealth in their future lives, we should encourage them to make offerings and be generous while they are alive. The Buddha said generosity is the cause of wealth, not burning papers.

Sometimes, we may advise our relatives, "Don't give so much. Then the family will not have." By encouraging them to be miserly while they are alive, we cause them to plant the seeds on their mind stream to be poor in their future lives. Also, we plant the same kind of seed on our own mind stream. On the other hand, if we encourage them to be generous and to avoid stealing and cheating others in business, then we are helping them to have riches.

If we want our loved ones to have a good rebirth, the best help we can give is to encourage them while they are alive to avoid the ten non-virtues and practice the ten virtues which are their opposites. These ten are killing, stealing, sexual misconduct, lying, slander, abuse, gossip, coveting others' possessions, maliciousness and wrong views. Instead, if we encourage them to lie to protect us or to cheat someone, we are helping them to create the cause for suffering rebirths. Should we spend hours gossiping with them, drinking and criticizing others, we are merely defeating our own purpose. Since we sincerely want them to be happy after death, we should help them abandon these destructive actions and practice constructive ones. We can encourage (not force) them to take the five precepts or even to become a monk or nun. That is really acting to benefit their future lives.

ATTACHMENT, DETACHMENT AND DESIRE

What is the difference between being attached to other people and loving them?

With attachment, we overestimate other people's qualities, thinking that they are better than they actually are. Also, we care about them because they please us: they give us presents, praise us, help and encourage us, etc. What we ordinarily call love is usually just attachment. With attachment, we do not see people for who they are and thereby develop many expectations of them: they should be like this, they should do that, etc. Then, when they do not live up to what we thought they were or should be, we are hurt, disillusioned, and blame them.

With genuine love, we care for other people and want them to be happy not because they please our ego and desires, but just because they exist. Real love does not expect anything from others in return. We accept people for who they are and still try to help them, but we are not concerned at all with how we will benefit from the relationship. Real love is not jealous and possessive. Rather, it is impartial and is shared with all beings.

If we are detached, is it possible to be with our friends and family?

Of course! Detachment does not mean rejection. With detachment, we no longer have unrealistic expectations of others, nor do we cling to them, thinking

we will be miserable when they are not around. Detachment is a calm, realistic, open and accepting attitude.
It is not hostile, paranoid and unsociable. Detachment
does not mean that we reject our friends and family:
it means we relate to them in a different way. When
we are not attached, our relationships with others
are harmonious, and in fact, we care more about
them.

Are all desires bad? What about the desire to attain nirvana or enlightenment?

This confusion occurs because we use the English
word "desire" as a translation for two different words.
In actual fact, there are different kinds of "desire."
The desire that gives us problems is the one that over-
exaggerates the good qualities of an object, person or
idea and clings to it. Such desire is a form of attachment. An example is being very emotionally dependent
on someone, and clinging to him/her. In actual fact,
the other person is not nearly as fantastic as our
misconceiving attachment is making him/her seem to be.

However, the desire that spurs us to make
preparation for future lives or to attain nirvana or
enlightenment is completely different. Here we are
accurately seeing better states of being and developing
a realistic aspiration to achieve them. There is no
misconception involved, nor is there clinging to the
desired result.

Can one be attached to Buddhism? What should we do if someone attacks our beliefs and criticizes the Dharma?

Each situation has to be regarded individually. However, in general, if we feel "They are criticizing my belief. They think I am stupid for believing that," it means we are clinging onto our beliefs. We are thinking "These beliefs are good because they are mine. If someone criticizes them, they are criticizing me." That is simply attachment and is not very productive. Such an attitude should be abandoned. We are not our beliefs. That others challenge our beliefs does not mean that we are stupid.

It is advantageous to be open to what others say. Let's not be attached to the name and label of our religion. We are seeking truth and happiness, aren't we, not just defense of a religion because it happens to be ours. The Buddha himself said we should check his teachings and not just believe in them blindly.

On the other hand, that does not mean that we automatically agree with everything other people say; we do not abandon our beliefs and adopt theirs indiscriminately. Whenever someone asks us a question that we cannot answer, it does not mean that the Buddha's teachings are wrong. It simply signifies that we do not know the answer and we need to learn and contemplate more. We should then go to knowledgeable Buddhists with these questions and think about the answers they give. When other people question our beliefs, they are helping us deepen our understanding of the Buddha's teachings by showing us what we do not understand well. This makes us study the Dharma and reflect on its meaning more deeply.

We do not need to defend our belief to someone else. If the person is asking with sincere interest to know the answer, if the person is open-minded and interested in impartial discussion, then talking with him/her can be mutually enriching. However, if someone really does not want a response, and just wants to poke verbal needles for the sake of antagonizing us or making us confused, then dialogue is impossible. There is no need to feel defensive in front of such a person — we do not have to prove anything to him. Even if we were to respond to his questions with perfect and logical arguments, he/she is not listening for he/she is deeply immersed in his/her own preconceptions. It is not useful to engage in conversation with such a person. Without being rude to him/her, we can still be quite firm in letting him/her know that we wish to be left alone.

WOMEN AND THE DHARMA

Can liberation and enlightenment be attained by both men and women?

According to the Vajrayana, yes. In the Theravadin and general Mahayana, it is believed that although one can attain liberation with a female body, to attain full enlightenment, one has to have a male body in the last rebirth. However, according to the tantric practice, both men and women can attain enlightenment equally. His Holiness the Dalai Lama repeatedly stressed this.

Why are there comparatively fewer ordained women practitioners, and why do they seem to be accorded less respect than the men?

In most cultures, women's activities are more restricted and their social position lower than men. So it was in ancient India, and thus Buddha designated that the women sit behind the men and be served after them. This pertains to social customs, and is not indicative of women's intelligence or capability. In fact, while the man is representative of the method aspect of the path to enlightenment, the woman is symbolic of the wisdom aspect!

Can women make offerings and prayers during menstruation? Can she meditate at that time?

Of course! Any notion that she cannot is mere superstition.

Is it harder for a woman to practice the Dharma than for a man?

That completely depends on the individual. For some women, their menstrual cycle causes many emotional changes. But they can learn to deal with that. After-all, men can be moody too! I believe that one of the principal things that could hold a woman back is her own limited self-concept and self-confidence. If we think that we cannot do something well, then we do not even try. What a waste of our human potential! As long as we are human beings with human intelligence, and have not only met the Dharma but also have all the necessary conditions to practice and attain realizations, then let's do it!

MONKS, NUNS AND LAY DEVOTEES

What are the benefits of taking ordination as a monk or nun? Is it necessary in order to practice the Dharma?

No, becoming a monk or nun is not necessary in order to practice the Dharma. To take ordination is an individual choice that each person must make for him/herself. Of course, there are many advantages to being ordained: by living within the precepts, one is constantly accumulating positive potential. As long as the person is not breaking the precepts, even if one is sleeping, one is continuously enriching one's mental continuum with positive potential. One also has more time and less distractions for practicing. With family obligations, much time and energy have to be spent taking care of the family. Children require much care, and it is difficult to meditate if they are playing or crying nearby. Someone who sees these as hindrances and who wants to pacify his/her mind and accumulate a rich store of positive potential, may decide to take ordination in order to have a better situation for practice.

How can a lay person practice the Dharma?

Those who wish to be lay Buddhists can practice the Dharma well by subduing their mind. It is needlessly downgrading one's own potential to think, "I am a lay person. To listen to teachings, to chant and to meditate is the work of monks and nuns. It is not my job. I just go to the temple, bow, make offerings and pray for the welfare of my family." These activities are good, but lay people are capable of a much richer spiritual life, in terms of both knowledge about Buddhism and integration of it into their daily life. It is very important that they attend Dharma talks and follow a series of teachings. By doing this, lay people will understand the real truth and beauty of the Dharma. Otherwise, they remain "joss stick Buddhists," and if someone asks them a question about Buddhism, they have difficulty in responding. That is a sad situation.

After hearing teachings, one should put them into practice as much as possible. A daily practice of chanting or meditating is excellent. Sometimes lay students say, "My day is so busy with work, family and social obligations. There is no time left to do a daily Dharma practice." This is a poor excuse, created by the lazy mind. There is always time to eat: we take care never to miss a meal. Just as we are so diligent and careful to nourish our body, and always find time to do so, so too should we be about nourishing our mind. After all, it is our mind that continues on to future lives, carrying with it all the karmic imprints of our actions, not our body. Dharma practice is not done for the Buddha's benefit, but for our own. The Dharma describes how to create the cause for happiness, and since we all want happiness, all of us should practice as much as we can.

Also, it is very advantageous and beneficial for lay disciples to take the five lay precepts for the duration of their life or take the eight precepts on special days, such as new and full moon days. In this way, much positive potential is created.

The responsibility for the existence and spread of the Buddha's teachings lies with both monks and nuns and lay disciples. If we see the value of the Buddha's teachings and want them to continue to exist and to flourish, then we have the responsibility to learn about them and to practice them ourselves according to our capabilities. There are many historical examples of lay people who have attained spiritual realizations. It is inspiring to learn about their lives and to emulate them.

Do people become monks and nuns to escape the harsh realities of life?

If someone becomes a monk or nun for this reason, he/she has an impure motivation, and such a person will not find ordained life satisfying. The causes of suffering are attachment, ignorance and hatred. These attitudes follow us everywhere. They do not need a passport to go with us to another country, nor are they left outside the monastery gate. As long as we have attachment, ignorance and hatred, we cannot escape problems, be we ordained or lay.

People who ask this question think that having a job, a mortgage and a family to care for are difficult tasks and constitute the "harsh reality of life." A harsher reality is to be honest with ourselves and to see our own wrong conceptions and harmful behavior. A harder job is to work to eliminate our anger, attachment and close-mindedness. A person chanting or sitting in silent meditation cannot show a skyscraper or a paycheck as the sign of his/her success, but that does not mean that that person is lazy and irresponsible. It takes much effort to change our detrimental habits of body, speech and mind; it is not an easy task to become a Buddha. Instead of "escaping reality," sincere practitioners are trying to discover it! Those people who chase after sense pleasures are the ones trying to escape reality, for they avoid looking at the reality of death and the functioning of cause and effect. In the Dharma sense, they are lazy, because they do not endeavour to subdue their attachment, anger and close-mindedness.

Some people think, "Only people who cannot make it 'in the real world' become monks and nuns. Maybe they have family problems, or they did not do well in school or they are poor and homeless. They go to the temple to live and take vows just to have a home and an occupation." Thinking in this way, some people look down upon those who are ordained. This is not correct. Should someone become a monk or nun for this reason, he/she does not have the correct motivation, and the masters who give ordination try to weed such people out. On the contrary, those who take ordination with a correct motivation have strong aspiration to develop their potential in order to subdue their mind and to help others.

Is a person who takes ordination being unfilial by leaving his/her family?

Not at all. On the contrary, people who sincerely want to make the world a better place through their religious practice are very filial. They see that by creating the causes for future good rebirths, by purifying and developing their minds, they will be able to guide others to lasting happiness through the path of the Dharma. They know that is of great benefit to their parents and of service to society. Although attaining high realizations may not occur in this very life, they have a broad vision and work for long-range happiness and benefit. A truly filial and dedicated child thinks, "If I continue with my worldly life, I will only create the causes for lower rebirths for myself and cause others to do the same. How can I help my parents in this and all future lives if I do that? Whereas if I engage in sincere practice of the Dharma, my own qualities will increase and I will be able to guide and help them in a better way and for a longer time."

That ordained ones leave the family life does not mean that they reject their family. Although they want to abandon the afflictive emotion of attachment towards their family, they still appreciate the kindness of their parents and care about them very much. Rather than confine their care to a few human beings, ordained ones seek to develop impartial love for all, and to consider all beings as part of their family.

How are parents to feel if their child becomes a monk or nun?

Very happy. It is a sign that they, as parents, have instilled in their child a sense of morality and care for others. Contrarily, some parents get upset if their child wants to become a monk or nun. They fear that the child will not be happy or will not have financial security. Some parents are angry, "We paid so much for your education. Who will take care of us when we are old if you are in a monastery? How unfilial!"

It is sad to see parents having this attitude. From their side, they mean well: they want their child to be happy. But material happiness and having a family, career and many possessions is not the only way to happiness. In fact, they bring new problems: we create negative actions to get them, we worry about not having enough and what will happen to what we do have. This is why Sakyamuni Buddha left his family and sensuous life at the palace in order to seek lasting and genuine happiness. Of course, his parents were upset too! But parents who really care about their child's happiness will be delighted if the child wants to practice the Dharma intensely, for such a practice will insure that the child will be happy at death time and in all future lives. With practice, their child can enjoy the bliss of liberation and enlightenment. A wise parent will care for the child's happiness, not only in this life but in all future time.

It is wise for parents to be aware of their own motivation. The Buddha's father wanted to be able to say, "My son is a king. He is highly regarded by the people in the country." Also, his parents were attached to their child and did not want to part from him. That is a natural reaction for parents to have. How ironic! Their son received more respect from people and greater fame throughout the ages by virtue of his spiritual practice. He would never have been that renown and highly regarded had he assumed the kingship of his land!

Parents who see the truth in Buddha's teachings will be delighted that their child takes ordination. The child's spiritual practice will benefit others — including the parents themselves — in the long run, even if obvious results are not displayed in this life. They will be pleased that their child is intelligent and sees the truth in the Dharma; they will be proud that he/she wants to live in pure morality, and they will be happy, as they see their child become rich in compassion and wisdom. Such parents do not feel as if they had lost their child. Rather, they rejoice that he/she can live his/her life in such a beneficial way.

Is taking ordination a painful sacrifice?

It should not be. We should not feel, "I really want to be able to do these things, but now I can't." Abandoning negative actions is not to be seen as a burden, but as a joy. Such an attitude comes from contemplating cause and effect.

When we take vows, be they the five precepts of a lay person or the vows of a monk or nun, we first generate the attitude, "I do not want to do these actions in any case. In my heart, I do not want to kill, steal, lie and so on." Sometimes we are weak in the actual situation and are tempted to do these things, but taking precepts gives us extra strength and determination not to do what we really do not want to do. For example, we may sincerely want to abandon killing. But when cockroaches are in our flat, we may be tempted to use insecticide. Having taken a precept of not killing, we remember that we do not want to kill. We are more mindful of our actions and have more strength and determination to confront and avert the afflictive emotions which could cause us to engage in negative actions. In such a way, precepts are liberating, not confining, for we free ourselves from the habitual tendency to follow the afflictive emotions and engage in detrimental actions.

Sometimes we encounter ordained ones and lay devotees who are bad-natured and difficult to get along with inspite of their religious practice. Why?

It takes time to change the mind. Dissolving our anger is not an easy process. We can understand that from our own experience: when we are habituated with losing our temper, it takes more than just saying, "I shouldn't do this" for us to stop. It needs consistent and correct practice. We have to be patient with ourselves, and similarly, we have to be patient with others. We are all on the path; we are all fighting the internal enemies of the afflictive emotions and the imprints of past actions. Sometimes we are strong in confronting them, other times we are carried away by anger, jealousy, attachment or pride. Sometimes we see our close-mindedness; other times we are blind to it. Judging and blaming ourselves when we succumb to the afflictive emotions does no good. Likewise, blaming and criticizing others when they do so is fruitless. Knowing how difficult internal transformation is ourselves, we should be patient also with others.

That practitioners are not perfect does not mean that the method the Buddha taught is not perfect. It means either that they do not practice it well, or their practice is not yet strong enough. It is extremely important in religious circles that people try to be harmonious and to accept each others' weaknesses. Our job is not to point fingers and say, "Why don't you practice better? Why don't you control your temper?" Our job is to think, "Why don't I practice better so their actions don't make me angry?" and "What can I do to help them?"

MEDITATION

What is meditation?

The Tibetan word for meditation is "gom." This has the same verbal root as the words to habituate or to familiarize. Meditation is habituating ourselves with positive, constructive and realistic attitudes. It is building up good habits of the mind. Meditation is not sitting in the full-vajra position, with an arrow-straight back and a holy expression on our face. Meditation is done with the mind. Even if the body is in perfect position, if the mind is running wild and thinking about objects of attachment, that is not meditation. With meditation, we transform our thoughts and views so that they are more compassionate and correspond to reality.

Can meditation be dangerous? Some people say you can go crazy from it. Is that true?

If we learn how to meditate from an experienced teacher who gives instruction in a reliable method, and if we follow these instructions correctly, there is no danger at all. Meditation is simply building up good habits of the mind. This we do in a gradual fashion; it is unwise to try to do an advanced practice without proper instruction, when we are beginners. However, if we practice a reliable path in a gradual fashion, we, too, can become Buddhas!

In order to meditate, we must first receive meditation instruction from a reliable teacher. Some people think they can invent their own way to meditate and that they do not need to learn from a knowledgeable teacher. This is very unwise. It is to our advantage to listen to teachings given by a reliable source like the Buddha. These teachings have been examined by scholars and practiced by skilled meditators who have attained results. In this way, we can establish that a lineage of teachings and meditation practice is valid and worthy to be practiced. These days many people teach meditation and spiritual paths, but we should check them well and not just excitedly jump into something. If the meditation practice is one taught by the Buddha and passed down in a pure lineage, we can trust it. Such a practice has not been made up on someone's whim.

How do we learn meditation? What kinds of meditation are there?

First, we listen to teachings and then deepen our understanding by checking and contemplating them. Then, we combine what we have learned with our mind stream through meditation. For example, we hear teachings on how to develop impartial love for all beings. Next, we check up and investigate if that is possible. We come to understand each step in the practice. Then, we build up this good habit of the mind by integrating it with our being; we try to experience the various steps leading to impartial love. That is meditation.

There are two general kinds of meditation: those designed to develop concentration, and ones to develop analytical ability and wisdom. The Buddha taught a wide variety of meditation techniques and the lineages of these are extant today. A simple meditation of watching the breath can be done to calm the mind and free it of the usual chatter. This helps us to be calmer in our daily life and not to worry so much. Other meditations help us control anger, attachment and jealousy by developing positive and realistic attitudes towards other people. There are purification meditations to cleanse the imprints of negative actions and to stop that nagging guilty feeling. In some meditations, we see through the fantasies we have about who we are and build up a realistic self-confidence and a positive self-image. These are just a few types of meditation.

What are the benefits of meditation?

By building up good habits of the mind in meditation, our daily life behavior gradually changes. Our anger is subdued, we are better able to make decisions and are less dissatisfied and restless. These results of meditation can be experienced now. But, we should always try to have a broader and more encompassing motivation to meditate than just our own present happiness. If we generate the motivation to meditate in order to make preparation for future lives, or to attain liberation from the cycle of constantly recurring problems, or to reach the state of full enlightenment for the benefit of all sentient beings, then naturally our mind will also be peaceful now. In addition, we will be able to attain those high and noble goals.

It is very beneficial to have a regular meditation practice, even if it is only for a short time each day.

66

Do not think, "I'm a working person. I can't meditate. That is the job of monks and nuns." Not at all! If meditation is helpful to us, we should make a time for it every day. Even if we do not want to meditate, it is important to keep some "quiet time" for ourselves each day: time when we sit and reflect upon what we do and why, time when we read a Dharma book or do some chanting. It is extremely important that we learn to like ourselves and are happy to be alone. Keeping aside some quiet time, preferably in the morning before the activities of the day are underway, is necessary, especially in modern societies where people are so busy. We always have time to nourish our bodies; we never skip a meal because we see it is important. Likewise, we should reserve time to nourish our mind and our inner being as well, because it too is important.

Can one get clairvoyant powers through practicing Buddhism? Is this a worthwhile goal to pursue?

Yes, one can, but that is not the principle goal of the practice. Some people get very excited over the prospect of having clairvoyance. "Wait until I tell my friends about this! Everyone will think I'm special and will come to ask me for advice. I'll be well-known and well-respected." What an egotistical motivation for wanting to be clairvoyant! If we still get angry and cannot control what we say, think and do, what use is it running after clairvoyance? It could even become a distraction to our practice because we get caught up in the excitement and the reputation. It is far more beneficial for this and future lives' happiness to concentrate on becoming a kind person who has an altruistic attitude.

Once a child asked me if I had clairvoyance. Could I bend a spoon through concentration? Could I stop a clock or walk through a wall? I told him no, and even if I could, what use would it be? Does that lessen the suffering in the world? The person whose spoon I ruined may suffer more! The point of our human existence is not to build up our ego but to develop a kind heart and a sense of universal responsibility working for world peace. Loving-kindness is the real miracle!

If one has a kind heart, then developing clairvoyant powers could be beneficial for others. High practitioners do not go around advertising their clairvoyance. In fact, most of them will deny it and will be very humble. The Buddha warned against public displays of clairvoyance unless it was necessary in order to benefit others. Humble people are actually more impressive than boastful ones: their serenity and respect for others shine through. Someone who has subdued pride, who has a loving-kindness attitude toward others, and who is developing his/her wisdom is someone we can trust. Such a person is working for the benefit of others, not for his/her own prestige and wealth. This person we can rely on.

STEPS ALONG THE PATH

Who is an arhat (arahat)? What is nirvana (nibbana)?

An arhat is someone who has eliminated the ignorance and afflictive emotions (anger, attachment, jealousy, pride, etc.) from his/her mind forever. In addition, he/she has purified all karma that could cause rebirth in the cycle of constantly recurring problems (samsara). This person abides in a state of peace, beyond all sorrow and suffering, called nirvana or liberation.

What is bodhi or enlightenment?

In addition to eliminating ignorance, afflictive emotions and karma from one's mind, a Buddha has also eliminated the stains of these defilements. Thus, a Buddha has purified all defilements and developed all of his/her qualities. The resultant state attained is called enlightenment.

What is a bodhisattva, a dedicated being?

A bodhisattva is a being who spontaneously and continuously has the wish to attain enlightenment for the benefit of sentient beings. By practicing the path, such a person will attain the state of Buddhahood.

There are different levels of bodhisattvas, according to their level of realization. Some are not yet free from the cycle of constantly recurring problems, while others are. The latter can then take birth in the world voluntarily, by the power of compassion, in order to help others. Buddhas can do this as well.

What is an arya, a superior or noble one?

This is a person who has direct realization of emptiness. Such a realization occurs before one becomes an arhat or Buddha, and it is by this wisdom realizing emptiness that one eliminates ignorance, afflictive emotions, karma, and their stains, thereby attaining liberation and enlightenment.

SELFLESSNESS

Do "selflessness" and "emptiness" mean the same thing?

Generally, they do.

What is the advantage of realizing selflessness or emptiness?

We are then able to cleanse our mind of all defilements and obscurations. At the moment, our mind is obscured by ignorance: the way we perceive and grasp ourselves and other phenomena as existing is not the way that they really exist. It is similar to a person who wears sunglasses all the time. Everything he sees appears dark and he thinks that that is the way they are. In fact, if he took his sunglasses off, he would find that actually they exist in a different way.

Another analogy to our ignorant view is a person who watches a movie and thinks that the people on the screen are real. He/she becomes very emotional and involved in the fate of the characters, and being attached to the hero, he/she is antagonistic towards the characters who disturb him. The person may even cry out, cringe, or jump up in his/her seat when the hero is harmed. In fact, that is not necessary at all, for there are no real people on the screen at all. They are only projections which are dependent on causes and conditions such as the film, the film projector and the screen. Realizing emptiness is analogous to understanding that the movie is empty of real people. Yet the appearance of the characters does exist, dependent on the film, screen and so forth. Thus, the person is still able to enjoy the film, but does not emotionally go up and down as the hero experiences various events.

By generating the wisdom which directly realizes emptiness, we perceive the mode in which we and other phenomena exist: they are empty of our fantasized projections on them — especially the projection of inherent existence. Having this wisdom realizing reality, we are freed from the bonds of ignorance that mis-conceives reality. Familiarizing our mind with emptiness, we gradually eliminate all ignorance, anger, attachment, pride, jealousy, and other afflictive attitudes from our mind. By doing so, we cease to create the destructive actions motivated by them. Freed from the influence of ignorance, afflictive emotions and the actions motivated by them, we are liberated from the causes of our problems, and thus the problems also cease. In other words, the wisdom realizing emptiness is the true path to happiness.

What does it mean to say, "All persons and phenomena are empty of true or inherent existence?"

It means that persons (like you and me) and all other phenomena (tables, etc.) are empty of our fantasized projections on them. One of the principle deceptive qualities that we project onto persons and phenomena is that they are inherently existent, that is, that they exist without depending on causes and conditions, parts, and the consciousness which conceives them and gives them a name. Thus, in our ordinary view, things appear to have some true or inherent nature, as if they were really there, as if we could find these real, independent entities if we searched for them. They appear to be there, independent of the causes and conditions that created them, independent of the parts of which they are made, and independent of the mind which conceives and gives them a name. This is the appearance of true or inherent existence and our mind grasps it as real.

However, when we examine analytically if things exist in this independent way as they superficially appear to, we find that they do not. They are empty of our fanta-sized projections onto them. Still, they do exist, but they exist dependently, for they rely on causes and conditions, on parts, and on the mind which conceives them and gives them a name.

If all people and phenomena are selfless or empty, does that mean that nothing exists?

No, phenomena and people still exist. After all, I am still here typing and you are still reading! Emptiness is not nihilism. Rather, people and phenomena are empty of our fantasized projections upon them. They lack what our wrong conceptions attribute to them. They do not exist in the way they appear to us at the present, but they do exist.

What is the best way to realize emptiness of inherent existence?

As this realization is difficult to gain and is an advanced stage of path, we develop our understanding slowly. The path to liberation and enlightenment is a gradual one, and we practice in steps. First we train in the elementary aspects of the path, such as imper-manence, refuge, love and compassion, and so forth. Then we listen to teachings on emptiness from a reliable and knowledgeable master. Contemplating and discussing these teachings, our understanding becomes clearer. Once we have a clear idea of the subject, we then begin to integrate it with our mind through meditation.

VAJRAYANA

What is Vajrayana?

Vajrayana, which is also called Tantrayana, is a subdivision of the Mahayana. It is based upon both the Theravadin and general Mahayana practices. Before entering into the Vajrayana, we must be well-trained in the thought definitely to emerge from the cycle of constantly recurring problems (renunciation), the heart dedicated to attaining enlightenment for the benefit of all sentient beings (bodhicitta), and the wisdom realizing the emptiness of inherent existence. Then we take an initiation from a qualified tantric master and protect the tantric vows and commitments that are received at the time of initiation. On the basis of this, we can receive instructions and engage in the Vajrayana meditation practice.

One technique used in the Vajrayana is visualizing ourself as the deity and our environment as the mandala or the environment of the deity. By visualizing in such a way, we transform our ordinary poor self-image into that of the deity and thus try to cultivate such noble qualities in our own mind stream. Vajrayana also contains techniques for transforming death, the intermediate state and rebirth into the body and mind of a Buddha. There are also special meditative techniques to develop calm abiding (samatha) as well as to make manifest an extremely subtle mind which, when realizing emptiness, becomes very powerful in quickly cleansing the defilements. It is for this reason that Vajrayana can bring enlightenment in this very lifetime to a qualified and well-trained disciple, who practices under the guidance of a fully-qualified tantric master.

Buddhist Tantra is not the same as Hindu Tantra. Nor is it some kind of practice of magic. Some people have written books about Vajrayana with incorrect information and interpretations. Therefore, if we wish to learn about this, it is important either to read books by a knowledgeable author or seek instruction from a qualified master.

What is an initiation? Why are there some teachings that are "secret"?

The purpose of initiation is to ripen our mind stream for the tantric practice by making a connection between the deity, who is a manifestation of the omniscient mind, and us. Initiation is not received by our body being in the room where an initiation is going on. Rather, we must meditate and do the visualizations that the master is describing. Initiation is not having a vase put on our head, or drinking blessed water, or getting a string to tie around our arm. It is ripening our own potential, through making a connection with a particular manifestation of the Buddha. This depends on our having a virtuous motivation and on concentrating and meditating during the initiation procedure.

After initiation, a sincere practitioner seeks instructions on how to do the practice. These instructions are not given before the initiation because the disciple's mind is not yet prepared to practice them. It is for this reason that they are "secret." It is not that the Buddha was miserly and did not want to share

the teachings, nor is the tantric practice like the posses-
sion of an exclusive club which jealously guards its
secrets. Rather, to ensure that those engaging in the
practice are properly prepared, tantric instruction is
given only to those who have received initiation. Otherwise, someone could misunderstand the symbolism
employed in the tantra or could engage in advanced
and complex practices without proper preparation and
instruction.

What does the imagery in tantric art mean?

Vajrayana deals a lot with transformation, and
therefore, symbolism is widely used. There are repre-
sentations of some deities, which are manifestations of
the Buddha, that are expressing desire or wrath. The
sexual imagery is not to be taken literally, according to
worldly appearances. In Vajrayana, deities in sexual
union represent the union of method and wisdom, the
two aspects of the path that need to be developed in
order to attain enlightenment. Wrathful deities are not
monsters threatening us. Their wrath is directed toward
ignorance and selfishness, which are our real enemies.
This imagery, when properly understood, shows how
desire and anger can be transformed and thereby
subdued. It has deep meaning, far beyond ordinary
lust and anger. We should not misinterpret it.

**What is the purpose of reciting mantras like "om
mani padme hung"? What does that mantra mean?**

Mantras are prescribed syllables to protect the mind.
What we want to protect our mind from are attachment,

anger, ignorance, and so on. When combined with the four opponent powers explained earlier, mantra recitation is very powerful in purifying negative karmic imprints on our mind stream. While we recite mantras, we should also be thinking and visualizing in a beneficial way so that we are building up constructive habits of the mind.

In the Vajrayana practice, mantras are recited in Sanskrit, rather than being translated into other languages. The reason for this is that there is a special beneficial energy or vibration that is induced by the sound of the syllables. While doing recitation, we can concentrate on the sound of the mantra, on its meaning, or on the accompanying visualizations that the master has taught.

"Om mani padme hung" is the mantra of the Buddha of Compassion, Avalokiteshvara (Kuan Yin, Chenresig). We may recite this mantra even if we have not received the oral transmission from a master, but it is more effective if the master first recites the mantra and we repeat it after him/her.

The entire meaning of the gradual path to enlightenment is contained in the six syllables of this mantra. "Om" refers to the body, speech and mind of the Buddhas, that is, what we want to attain by our practice. "Mani" means jewel, and refers to all the method aspects of the path: the wish definitely to emerge from the cycle of constantly recurring problems, compassion, generosity, morality, patience, joyous effort and so on. "Padme" (pronounced pay may) means lotus, and refs to the wisdom aspect of the path. By uniting both method and wisdom in a combined practice, we can purify our mind stream of all its defilements and develop all of our potentials. "Hung" (sometimes written "hum") refers to the mind of all the Buddhas.

Recitation of "om mani padme hung" is very effective for purifying the mind and for developing compassion. It can be recited out loud or silently, and at any time. For example, if we are waiting in a queue, instead of getting impatient and angry, we can mentally recite this mantra and think compassionate thoughts.

SPONSORS

The publication of this booklet was made possible by the kind help of the following people:

Metalloy Trading Co.
Amelia Teo
Angeline Lim
Ho Kim Eng
Tan Aik Huat
Tan Hup Cheng
Yeo Soo Hwa
Julie Sim
Sian Teck Tng
Yeo Choon Siang
Mr. Goh
Thubten Jampa
Tam Bee Larn
Lillian Lee
Chan Jer Luang
Mr. and Mrs. Two Teck Cheow
Lee Yong Seng
Lee Jun Qiao
Lee Mei Yi
Tan Poh Geok
Ng Ah Bak
Lim Eng Tiong
Lim Lay Guat
Tan Poh Beng
Foong Wan Har
Tan Cheng Chuan
Tan Bee Kiat
Tan Beng Hock and family
Tan Sah Nia
Lim Ah Hong
Tan Twe Joo
Yew Khow Ngoh

Molly Sim G.H.
Ong Kah Tin
Sek Meng Liang
Pang Kim Hoon
Sim Kim Choon
Sim Kim Yeow
Sim Tuay Hia
Sim Siang Kiang
Helen Ong
Ho Sai Kheng
Koh Hui Ngin
Tan Hwee Eng
Chong Kim Choon
Ng Kim Tee
Lee Muey Soon
Tan Ngoh Nia
Peggy Lim
Ng Chee Huat
Ng Kwang Liang
Lim Kim Swee
Oo Guat Chow
Cheng
P.C. Wong
Lim Kim Sim
Tan Kwang Meng
Marianne Ng Wai Chee
Ang Teck Hock
Tan Boon Leng
Mah Tuck Cheong
Ruby Cheah
Richard Masacorale

May all beings generate the path to enlightenment in their minds!